Within the Glass

Within the Glass

Anna Chatterton

Within the Glass
first published 2017 by
Scirocco Drama
An imprint of J. Gordon Shillingford Publishing Inc.

Scirocco Drama Editor: Glenda MacFarlane
Cover design by Terry Gallagher/Doowah Design Inc.
Author Photo by Dahlia Katz
Production photos by Cylla von Tiedemann
Printed and bound in Canada on 100% post-consumer recycled paper.

We acknowledge the financial support of the Manitoba Arts Council and The Canada Council for the Arts for our publishing program.

For professional or amateur production rights, please contact
Ian Arnold, Catalyst TCM
#312 – 100 Broadview Ave.
Toronto, ON Canada
M4M 3H3
phone: 416-568-8673
Email: ian@catalysttcm.com

Library and Archives Canada Cataloguing in Publication

Chatterton, Anna, author
Within the glass / Anna Chatterton.

A play.
ISBN 978-1-927922-32-3 (softcover)

I. Title.

PS8605.H3925W58 2017 C812'.6 C2017-900711-4

J. Gordon Shillingford Publishing
P.O. Box 86, RPO Corydon Avenue, Winnipeg, MB Canada R3M 3S3

For my mother, Elizabeth Susan Gertsman Chatterton

Anna Chatterton

Anna Chatterton is a librettist, playwright, and performer. Anna's plays include *Quiver* (Nightwood Theatre, Uno Festival, Playwrights Canada Press 2018,) and *Within the Glass* (Tarragon Theatre MainSpace.) She is a Playwright-in-Residence at Tarragon Theatre and Nightwood Theatre, and is in the playwrights unit at Alberta Theatre Projects.

Anna also writes and performs with the acclaimed feminist theatre collective Independent Aunties (with Evalyn Parry and Karin Randoja). The Aunties have created six shows together (co-written by Anna and Evalyn Parry) including *Clean Irene and Dirty Maxine* (Buddies in Bad Times Theatre, SummerWorks Award for Best New Play,) *Frances, Mathilda* and *Tea* (Theatre Passe Muraille,) *Breakfast* (Buddies in Bad Times Theatre and the Theatre Centre, three Dora Mavor Moore Award nominations,) and *Gertrude and Alice* (Buddies in Bad Times Theatre, Dora Mavor Moore Award nominations for Outstanding New Play and Outstanding Ensemble.) Anna was also honoured with a Toronto Theatre Critics Award for her role as Alice. *Gertrude and Alice* will be published by Playwrights Canada Press.

As a librettist Anna's work includes *Swoon* (Canadian Opera Company,) *Rocking Horse Winner* (Tapestry Opera,) *Crush* (COC and The Banff Centre,) and *The Man Who Married Himself* (Toronto Masque Theatre.) Anna works frequently with composer Juliet Palmer's company Urbanvesse; their work includes includes *Voice-Box* (World Stage / Harbourfront Centre,) *Stitch* (Theatre Centre,) and *Sweat* (Center for Contemporary Opera) in Brooklyn, NY. Anna and Juliet were nominated for a Dora Mavor Moore Award for Outstanding New Opera.

NOW magazine named Anna one of Toronto's Top Ten Theatre Artists of 2016 and she has been nominated three times for the K.M. Hunter Award for Theatre. Anna has her MFA in Creative Writing from the University of Guelph, and a BFA in Theatre Performance from Concordia University.

Acknowledgements

Within the Glass was developed through the Playwrights Unit, and subsequently in residence at Tarragon Theatre, with support from the Ontario Arts Council as well as the Toronto Arts Council.

Director Andrea Donaldson and I worked closely on this play and one couldn't ask for a more perfect director/writer relationship. I am eternally grateful for our joyful and intense artistic collaboration on this play and others in the works. Literary Manager Andrea Romaldi and Artistic Director Richard Rose also provided invaluable, insightful dramaturgy—and an additional deep thank you to Richard Rose for believing in the play.

Within the Glass was also developed at the Banff Centre for the Arts Playwrights Colony, and through the University of Guelph MFA program in Creative Writing—in both instances Colleen Murphy was a treasured mentor, and I am continually inspired and grateful to her. Judith Thompson is also my hero and a kind champion, and to both these geniuses and strong women I owe a great deal.

Deep gratitude to the talented, smarty-pants actors who performed the premiere production at Tarragon Theatre: Paul Braunstein, Nicola Correia-Damude, Philippa Domville and Rick Roberts. Your feedback was integral. And thank you to the actors who developed the play along the way: Tom Barnett, Liisa Repo Martell, Elizabeth Saunders, Kristen Thompson, David Jansen, Kevin Bundy, Severn Thompson, Claire Armstrong, Richard Zeppieri, Sasa Brown, Tracey L. Ferencz, Trevor Leigh, David McIlwraith.

To my other friends and artistic consultants/supporters: Evalyn Parry, Karin Randoja, Soraya Peerbaye, Suzanne Robertson, Ayelet Tsabari, Andrea Syrtash, Chris Warren, James Rolfe, Juliet Palmer, Sasha Wentges and Kelly Thornton.

The Tarragon Playwrights Unit—Andrew Kushnir, Deborah Pearson, Ravi Jain, d'bi young Anitafrika.

To all the blogs I followed, filled with women whose hearts were broken and bodies scarred from their years of struggling with infertility, and yet were there to provide support to any women who needed it—thank you.

Thank you as well to Glenda MacFarlane for choosing to publish this play and to Scirocco Drama and J. Gordon Shillingford Publishing.

Finally, thank you to life partner Jim Ruxton and our feisty daughter Frida, who was born in the middle of this play's development process—thank you forever.

Playwright's notes

This play is loosely based on a true story that I read about in the news. When I first read the story, I contemplated the two terrible choices the woman carrying the child was given, and I was plagued by one question: *What would I do*? I was inspired by the image of two mothers desperately fighting for one baby, which then expanded to two couples fighting for one baby. Though the law in Ontario asserts that the fetus belongs to the genetic parents, my play still begs the question: whose child is it? What makes a mother; what makes a parent? So many couples struggle with infertility, and this nightmarish dilemma is an example of what modern-day science has given us.

Production History

Within the Glass received its premiere at Tarragon Theatre in the Mainspace from January 6 to February 14, 2016 with the following cast:

Scott .... Paul Braunstein
Linda .... Nicola Correia-Damude
Darah .... Philippa Domville
Michael .... Rick Roberts

Directed by Andrea Donaldson
Set & Costume Design: Julie Fox
Sound Design: Mike Rinaldi
Lighting Design: Rebecca Picherack
Stage Manager: Natasha Bean-Smith
Assistant Director: Viktor Lukawski
Apprentice Stage Manager: Jacki Brabazon
Script Coordinator: Ali Joy Richardson

Linda (Nicola Correia-Damude) relaxes after voraciously eating. Scott (Paul Braunstein) makes sure she is all right, Darah (Philippa Domville) tries not to be jealous, and Michael (Rick Roberts) is enamoured.

Michael (Rick Roberts) and Scott (Paul Braunstein) have a man-to-man.

Michael (Rick Roberts) and Darah (Philippa Domville) get a moment alone.

Michael (Rick Roberts) gives Linda (Nicola Correia-Damude) a foot massage, while Darah (Philippa Domville) and Scott (Paul Braunstein) watch.

Encouraged by Michael (Rick Roberts), Darah (Philippa Domville) tries to feel her baby moving inside Linda (Nicola Correia-Damude), while Scott (Paul Braunstein) looks on.

Michael (Rick Roberts) embraces Linda (Nicola Correia-Damude) and Scott (Paul Braunstein) after Linda agrees to give them their baby. Darah (Philippa Domville) gets in on the hug.

Characters

DARAH .... forty-four, married to Michael
MICHAEL ....mid-to-late forties, married to Darah
LINDA .... thirty-six, married to Scott, 19 weeks pregnant
SCOTT.................................. early forties, married to Linda

Setting

Toronto. Evening. Darah and Michael's home.
All of the action takes place in their living room, which extends to a dining room with a beautifully set table. There is also a hallway with a door to a powder room.

Abbreviations

IUI *(Intrauterine Insemination):* a fertility treatment that involves placing sperm inside a woman's uterus to facilitate fertilization.

IVF *(In Vitro Fertilization):* the process by which an egg is fertilized by sperm outside the body in vitro ("in glass").

Act I

DARAH and MICHAEL are sitting on the couch in their living room, in silence.

DARAH: If they do this—

MICHAEL: They're going to do it.

DARAH: We can't assume. I just can't assume and then if they don't—

MICHAEL: If we think negatively—

DARAH: Let me just let me say what I was going to say. If—

MICHAEL: When—

DARAH: When…they do this, when it's all for sure, I promise I will call my mom every day.

MICHAEL: Really? Every day?

DARAH: Every day. That's a promise. If they do this—

MICHAEL: No more ifs.

DARAH: You have to promise something too. Something big. It's our last chance. …Your dad.

MICHAEL: No. Something else, there's plenty of—

DARAH: Not every day, just one call. It has to be big, Michael. That's how it works. If you don't promise, and they say no, I'll always wonder, I will. I can't help it.

MICHAEL: I'll call, tomorrow, tomorrow I'll call.

DARAH: Thank you. And I'll call my mom every day from now on. Every day.

(*Beat.*) Is my hair okay?

MICHAEL: You look beautiful.

DARAH: I wasn't sure if I should wear it up or down or…

MICHAEL: It's perfect…do you think I should have worn a tie?

DARAH: No. It's too formal. It will give the wrong impression.

MICHAEL: But what if he's wearing a tie?

DARAH: No one wears ties to dinner at home on the weekend. It's casual formal. You don't want him to think you're a workaholic who can't take a night off.

MICHAEL: But it's a business dinner, it is business of sorts. Maybe I should, just in case, I can always take it off.

DARAH: No, no, it will look wrong, it will look stiff, right off the bat, it will set everything on the wrong foot, it's things like that, small things that could change their mind, it's so fragile, it's that fragile.

(Beat.)

They're not coming.

MICHAEL: Try to relax…

DARAH: No. No. I knew it. Late means they're not going to do it.

MICHAEL: They're coming from the east end, the highway's always jammed.

DARAH: No, we'll hear from the lawyer tomorrow.

MICHAEL: *(Checks the time.)* It's only ten minutes. Worry at a half hour.

DARAH: I just can't bear it any longer. I almost wish they weren't coming.

MICHAEL: Have some wine, let's relax.

DARAH: I can't start a glass of wine before they get here. They'll think I'm a drinker.

MICHAEL: So hide the glass in the kitchen.

DARAH: They'll smell it on my breath.

He strokes her back.

DARAH: Careful of my hair. Ow.

MICHAEL: Did you hear a car door? I heard a car door slam.

DARAH: *(Listens.)* I didn't hear anything.

She runs to the window.

MICHAEL: Don't look.

DARAH: I'll just peek.

MICHAEL: No, they'll see you.

DARAH checks the room.

DARAH: The tzatziki, get the tzatziki—fridge, second shelf.

MICHAEL rushes to the kitchen, she peeks through the crack of the gauze curtain.

DARAH: Hurry!

MICHAEL rushes in with the dip, hands it to her, starts to go to the door.

Wait, wait. Michael. I'm not…I can't…Oh god, I just…

The doorbell rings.

MICHAEL: We can do this.

MICHAEL pauses, then opens the door.

MICHAEL: Hello, hey, come on in, Linda?

LINDA: Yes…Michael?

MICHAEL: Great to meet you. And Scott?

SCOTT: How's it going.

MICHAEL: Welcome, this is my wife, Darah.

DARAH: Hello, Linda, hello, Scott, welcome to our home, thank you so much for coming.

LINDA: We're late. My apologies. Traffic was…

MICHAEL: Not at all. Our pleasure, really. Great to have you here.

DARAH: We're just so—relieved—to finally meet you. You both look wonderful.

MICHAEL: Darah! Let them come in—I'll take your coats…

SCOTT: We're not staying long.

MICHAEL: Oh…

LINDA: (*Giving MICHAEL her coat.*) We can stay long enough to take off our coats, Scott.

SCOTT: (*To MICHAEL.*) I'm okay.

MICHAEL: Sure, sure, can I get you a glass of wine?

DARAH: I did make dinner…if you're hungry…Coq au vin, you'll love it. I mean, if you want some, that is…Please don't feel like you have to or anything…but if you're hungry…or not…

LINDA: Sounds wonderful. (*To SCOTT.*) Give Michael your coat, Scott…if they made us dinner…

SCOTT: That's chicken, right?

DARAH: It's capon, it's so delicious.

SCOTT: Linda's vegetarian.

DARAH: Oh my god. I feel terrible, I should have asked.

LINDA: Please, don't worry about it. It doesn't matter.

SCOTT: Anyway, we aren't here to eat.

DARAH: No please, it's no trouble I can just whip up a pasta or I think we might have some tofu…I'm so / sorry.

MICHAEL: We actually don't eat a lot of meat.

DARAH: We never eat red meat.

MICHAEL: Well, for starters, why don't we all sit down and have a drink?

DARAH: Yes, please sit? *(To LINDA.)* I've been so looking forward to meeting you. Stay a while. Please.

LINDA: *(Looks at SCOTT.)* Of course. We came all the way here right?

MICHAEL: Red or white, Scott?

LINDA: He'll have red.

SCOTT: Like the lady said…

DARAH: (*To LINDA.*) Would you like a Perrier? Or we have many kinds of juice—pomegranate, mango, lychee, or we have Limonata San Pellegrino?

MICHAEL: Or maybe you want a little wine?

DARAH looks at him aghast.

LINDA: Perrier is perfect, thank you.

DARAH: Perrier, wonderful.

MICHAEL: I'll get it.

DARAH: Thank you, darling.

MICHAEL exits to the kitchen.

Did you find the house okay?

SCOTT: Yeah, fine.

LINDA: It's a beautiful home.

DARAH: Thank you so much, we like it. We planned for a family, so ours is a four bedroom. It's a lot of house for just two.

Slight awkward pause. MICHAEL comes back in with the drinks. He hands wine to SCOTT.

MICHAEL: Here you go, sir.

SCOTT: Thanks.

MICHAEL: So nice to finally meet you.

MICHAEL hands a glass with Perrier to LINDA and a wine glass to DARAH.

LINDA: Sorry we took so long.

MICHAEL: Not at all, not at all.

DARAH: Please, have some tzatziki. And the pita's fresh. The bakery down the street is run by a lovely Greek family. We buy from them.

SCOTT tries it.

Do you like it?

SCOTT: Not bad.

MICHAEL: They make the tzatziki. It's a real mom-and-pop joint.

DARAH: *(To LINDA.)* Please, try a taste.

LINDA tries it.

It's sheep. Yogurt. Sheep yogurt. Family recipe straight from Greece.

LINDA: Mmm…it's very good.

DARAH: They go to a farm for the yogurt. They have pictures up in the bakery, of the sheep. They carry wonderful olive oil and the olives are from them too, they go to Greece every winter and bring it back with them. We're addicted.

MICHAEL: George and Martina, they've had their shop for twenty years. Sweet couple. We like to support our local shops.

LINDA: It's so thick.

DARAH: We have more in the fridge, I'll give you some to take home.

LINDA: Oh no…

DARAH: I insist. It's very healthy. Lots of garlic.

LINDA: Well, thanks.

DARAH: Our pleasure.

SCOTT gulps down some wine, looks at LINDA.

LINDA: (*Gesturing to the wall.*) That's a lovely painting.

MICHAEL: You like it? I've never been sure about it.

DARAH: I've always loved it.

LINDA: Who is it?

MICHAEL: Sorry?

LINDA: Who's the artist?

MICHAEL: Oh, I don't know, do you know honey?

DARAH: No…it's no one famous or anything…

MICHAEL: There must be a signature…maybe on the back?

DARAH: We can take it off the wall and look…

LINDA: Oh, that's okay, I just wondered.

MICHAEL: So, what do you guys do? I meant to ask.

DARAH: It seems so strange, we don't know anything about you…

SCOTT: Well, I'm a writer.

DARAH: Oh! I love to read. Do you write novels?

SCOTT: No.

DARAH: Oh.

LINDA: Scott writes poetry. He's an incredible poet.

DARAH: Poetry. Isn't that fantastic.

MICHAEL: Is it hard to get published these days? People don't buy books as much, do they?

SCOTT: Well, it's not like it used to be—

LINDA: He's being modest, he does very well. His last manuscript was picked up by the biggest publishing house in the country.

SCOTT: But he's right that it's not like it used to be.

LINDA: But that hasn't stopped you from being published. Or getting residencies and grants. Scott has taught all over the world.

DARAH: Isn't that marvelous.

MICHAEL: We'll have to check out some of your books.

DARAH: Yes, we definitely will. God, I can't even remember the last time I read a poem. University maybe? (*Beat.*) Michael works in investment banking.

SCOTT: No kidding? A banker?

MICHAEL: Yes sir.

LINDA: Is it as cut-throat as we hear?

MICHAEL: 'Tis a very sharp blade.

LINDA: I wouldn't have the stomach for it.

DARAH: He's got abs of steel.

MICHAEL: And Darah manages a company that makes computer games.

SCOTT: Really?

LINDA: Do you like playing them?

DARAH: Oh no, I hate them. That's why I accepted the position.

SCOTT: Because you hate them?

DARAH: It helps maintain perspective. It's great, you know, challenging, stressful…and the benefits and mat leave are unbelievable.

SCOTT: No mat leave for artists, eh, Linda?

LINDA: But a wide open schedule.

MICHAEL: (*To LINDA.*) You're an artist? Like paintings and drawing?

LINDA: I do a broad range in my practice.

MICHAEL: A professional artist, that's very impressive.

DARAH: I can only draw stick figures.

LINDA: Everyone is born an artist.

DARAH: Not me.

LINDA: When our daughter was six months I did an installation with her—and she played to the crowd, completely unselfconscious. We are all born that way.

SCOTT: It was a big hit, she got tons of press. She gave taste samples of her breast milk.

MICHAEL: You're kidding, really?

SCOTT: Yeah, she did.

DARAH: You have a daughter?

LINDA: Yes, Maya. She's eight.

DARAH: We didn't know. What a beautiful name, Maya.

LINDA: Thank you.

DARAH: Naturally or IVF?

SCOTT: We were lucky the first time. Unplanned too, so…

DARAH: Isn't that wonderful. I find it amazing anyone gets pregnant naturally.

LINDA: Do you have any children?

DARAH: No. Not yet.

MICHAEL: Did people actually drink your breast milk?

LINDA: Of course. It was pasteurized. There were the usual perverts who just came to ogle my breasts, but lots of people were just curious to taste it.

MICHAEL: What did it taste like?

SCOTT: Coconut milk. It was tasty.

LINDA: All the curries I was eating. So far this time, I haven't had any odd cravings. Except fruit. I could eat fruit all day long.

DARAH: I made a red velvet cake for dessert but I'll serve it with fruit.

LINDA: Mmm…I love red velvet cake.

DARAH: You do? I'm delighted.

SCOTT: We'll have to leave well before dessert.

DARAH: Oh, I hope not…

MICHAEL: Can I top you up, Scott?

SCOTT: I'm driving.

LINDA: I'll drive home, Scott.

SCOTT: You hate driving on the highway.

LINDA: We can weave through town, at night it'll be quick.

SCOTT: *(Under.)* How long are we here for then?

LINDA: Regardless, I'll drive.

MICHAEL offers SCOTT the wine, he nods.

LINDA: Thank god the first trimester is finally over, the nausea—I barely ate, I was sick all day long.

DARAH: Oh you poor thing.

LINDA: I'd try to go out, get something done and it would creep up on me again. Why is it just called morning sickness? And so tired…

SCOTT: Yeah, uh, it wasn't the pregnancy that made you comatose for days on end.

LINDA: Well…no, but…

MICHAEL: We know how difficult this must be, for both of you.

DARAH: We've been a mess, too.

MICHAEL: This whole ordeal has been…

SCOTT: It's been murder.

MICHAEL: Our lawyer is going to make sure the clinic is properly punished.

DARAH: I just want them to be shut down, immediately.

LINDA: I agree.

MICHAEL: What we've been put through is totally unacceptable.

SCOTT: Though, given the game we're playing, you have to expect something like this might happen.

DARAH: Game? You call this a game?

SCOTT: It's a gamble. Gambling's a game.

LINDA: Saying that is forgiving them.

DARAH: These are medical professionals, dealing with life—the precious lives of our embryos. Our future children, our future family. They should be triple, quadruple checking what they are doing.

SCOTT: Even with the most sophisticated technology, humans will still make mistakes.

MICHAEL: But they never warned us that something like this might happen. If we had known this type of mistake was possible, we might have thought twice before proceeding.

SCOTT: Really?

MICHAEL: We weren't given any indication—

SCOTT: So if they did you would have turned around and walked out? No dice, no baby, no way? Accepted what your bodies were telling you?

MICHAEL: Well…

SCOTT: Because that's the risk you take when you play with nature. Surely it occurred to you that you have no control, we are totally at their mercy.

DARAH: This wasn't just a mistake, it was negligence.

LINDA: The doctor told me I should terminate the next day, he said it was the best thing to do. He was insistent. I couldn't move.

DARAH: Dr. Quilter? Dr Quilter said that?

LINDA: Yes.

MICHAEL: I can't believe he said you should terminate.

DARAH: What right does he have, telling you what to do?

SCOTT: But he was right.

DARAH: I beg your pardon? What do you mean he was right?

SCOTT looks at LINDA. Pause.

LINDA: I've been trying to move past my anger at the clinic and just focus on the pregnancy.

SCOTT: What?

MICHAEL: That's great, we appreciate positivity.

DARAH: Sorry, does that mean…

LINDA: I'd like to discuss our options.

SCOTT: Options? Linda—

MICHAEL: What are you thinking about, Linda? We're happy to discuss options.

DARAH: We were so glad you wanted to meet in person.

SCOTT: *(Under.)* What's going on, Linda?

MICHAEL: And grateful you came to talk things through.

LINDA: Well, we appreciate you inviting us / into your beautiful home. There's been too many other people in the way, the lawyers, the clinic…

SCOTT: *(Under.)* Linda…

DARAH: I agree, really it's so personal, it's between us, just us four.

SCOTT: Linda, can I please speak with you in private?

MICHAEL: Hold on—talk to us, Linda, say anything you need to say, we're ready to hear what you've been thinking.

SCOTT: Linda, are you hearing me? Linda? Hello?

LINDA: *(Ignoring SCOTT.)* Well, the one thing that hasn't been put on the table is adoption.

SCOTT: What the fuck?

DARAH: I'm sorry, I'm confused, do you mean, did we consider adopting? Before…?

LINDA: I was given two choices, hand over the baby or terminate, how can those be the only choices?

SCOTT: That's why we're here, Linda? To say it in person? Closure?

DARAH: Closure? What closure, are you saying…what are you saying? Adoption? Closure? I don't understand. I really don't understand.

MICHAEL: Let's calm down here—Linda, where were you?

LINDA: I would like to adopt this baby.

DARAH: / What?

SCOTT: What the fuck are you talking about Linda?

LINDA: It's the only way I can live with what has happened.

SCOTT: You insisted on telling them in person that you were going to terminate.

DARAH: Terminate? You came here to tell us that you were…Michael…

MICHAEL: But that's not what you're saying right, Linda? You don't want to terminate? You want this little baby to live.

SCOTT: Little baby?

LINDA: Yes.

SCOTT: Okay, this is, this is / fucked up. Uh…

MICHAEL: Great, wonderful.

DARAH: I fail to see what is wonderful here, Michael.

MICHAEL: We can work with this—we're on the same page, we all want the baby to live, that's, that's a good first step.

SCOTT: No! We aren't on the same page at all, okay, we're in a different book, okay, we're speaking another language entirely.

MICHAEL: We're having a dialogue, an open dialogue. We can all state how we feel and—

SCOTT: Okay, I feel betrayed, uh, hung out to dry. Linda?

DARAH: But—but—the baby, the baby belongs to us, we want our baby, it's our baby.

LINDA: I don't see it that way.

SCOTT: So you lied, you lied to me.

LINDA: I had no choice.

SCOTT: You could have not lied, hey? How 'bout that?

DARAH: Everyone agrees. The doctors, the provincial courts, the lawyers, the law is on our side.

LINDA: Just in this province. In other provinces, in many states, and countries the birth mother is considered the mother.

DARAH: It's our DNA. Legally we have the right to our own flesh and blood. DNA wins out.

LINDA: What's legal isn't necessarily ethical.

DARAH: But it's completely immoral to expect parents to give up their own flesh and blood.

LINDA: But you have no connection to this baby at all.

DARAH: Are you crazy? It's my egg.

MICHAEL: Okay, okay, we were all placed in an immoral situation, we're all compromised.

SCOTT: Yeah, uh, we're beyond compromised. We're fucked.

LINDA: Look, when they told me what happened, I assumed I would miscarry. That my womb would reject the foreign body. But it just kept growing.

SCOTT: Jesus—fuck, Linda, let's go.

LINDA: My body is embracing it. Motherhood begins with pregnancy, I am mothering this baby, it's the first act of nurturing. Even though it's not my DNA.

DARAH: But we intended on having this child.

LINDA: So did we.

DARAH: I just don't understand. You came here expecting we would agree for you to adopt our baby?

SCOTT: No—fuck no.

LINDA: This baby growing inside me…

DARAH: My baby…

SCOTT: Fetus, it's a fetus.

LINDA: We are connected, we are in relationship every single moment of the day.

SCOTT: Of course you are—that's what the female body does—it grows a fetus.

LINDA: It's way beyond that. I'm talking about an emotional connection. Mother and child. Mommy and baby.

DARAH: But it's not your child. It's my child. Our child. I'm the mommy.

LINDA: Nature is very powerful. All my mothering instincts kicked in immediately. Protect this baby at all costs.

DARAH: And we appreciate that you are protecting our baby.

MICHAEL: Yes.

DARAH: Please understand, we are so grateful / that you have been taking such care.

MICHAEL: So grateful, so so grateful.

LINDA: My heart is attached. I am in love with this baby.

SCOTT: Okay, this is—

DARAH: In love with my baby?

LINDA: The baby I am growing.

SCOTT: Because you let it get this far. If you had just—

LINDA: The fact is, I'm the one who got pregnant. (*To DARAH.*) I'm sorry to bring this up, but it has to be pointed out that you didn't become pregnant from our embryo.

DARAH: That has nothing to do with it.

LINDA: Without me, this baby would not exist.

DARAH: You don't know that.

MICHAEL: You know what, it's best just not to go down this road okay? None of us know what would have happened if things had gone the way they were supposed to. Scott was right, we all know what a gamble it is.

SCOTT: See? The miracles of science.

LINDA: It's not a miracle, it's nature.

SCOTT: A miracle is an act defying the laws of nature. Which it was. What happened would be impossible if it weren't for technology. If we could just take no for an answer, this wouldn't have happened.

DARAH: What do you mean take no for an answer?

MICHAEL: He is right.

DARAH: Michael—

MICHAEL: *(To LINDA.)* It is a miracle that this baby is growing inside your body. We have been hoping and praying for years for an embryo to take and we don't know why or how but for some reason this time, our embryo survived.

DARAH: But it's not fair, I wasn't even given the chance to see if the embryo would take in my body.

MICHAEL: And that's the tragedy, but the celebration is… the embryo is thriving!

DARAH: But it was our miracle embryo, our genetics.

LINDA: My body is behaving naturally. It doesn't know it's not my genetics, it's growing a baby.

SCOTT: It isn't a baby, it's a fetus!

DARAH: Fetus?

SCOTT: Fetus is the accurate term. Medically it isn't considered a baby until birth.

MICHAEL: That's fair.

DARAH: You're just talking about semantics. To you it's a fetus, to us it's a baby. (*To LINDA.*) A helpless little baby trapped in your body.

LINDA: It's not trapped. It's flourishing inside of me.

SCOTT: It's only the size of a tomato.

LINDA: Actually, it's as big as a mango.

SCOTT: Okay, a large tomato.

DARAH: It's still a growing being.

SCOTT: It couldn't survive in the world as is. Semantics become a moral measure in this debate.

MICHAEL: But we aren't debating, no one is up in arms here. Can we at least celebrate that it's miraculous, to get this far along…I mean we're at nineteen weeks now, that's incredible.

SCOTT: This isn't a celebration. We shouldn't even be here. We shouldn't have to know each other exists.

MICHAEL: *(To LINDA.)* I just want to acknowledge that it was incredibly strong of you to carry on with the pregnancy.

LINDA: I had to, I didn't feel I had a choice, and I'm sending it so much love, every day, all day.

SCOTT: / That's—

MICHAEL: That's beautiful.

DARAH: Michael.

MICHAEL: We both appreciate you being so loving.

LINDA: That's just how it is when you're pregnant. Full of love. I can't imagine being separated from this little being inside me. And you shouldn't expect me to.

SCOTT: It shouldn't have gone this far, but you just kept stalling, and now—

DARAH: Do you have any idea how long we've been waiting for an embryo to take? Six years. Six years. Ten IUI's. Five IVF cycles. Countless embryos died in my womb. I have over twenty ghosts haunting me. Defected, abnormal, incomplete embryos. Empty sacs now absorbed by my body. And all they can tell us is that we have "unexplained infertility."

MICHAEL: Darah, please, we can discuss this calmly, we don't have to get so riled up.

DARAH: She was coming here to tell us she was going to terminate. She's asking to adopt, for god's sake. Aren't you upset?

LINDA: I wasn't going to terminate. I was never going to terminate.

SCOTT: You sure had me fooled. I'm the fool.

MICHAEL: Okay okay let's just—I'm sure we can work something out.

LINDA: (*To SCOTT.*) You would never have agreed to come.

SCOTT: For very good reasons, fuck's sake, adopt? I don't want this kid. It has nothing to do with me. I didn't do anything, I didn't contribute anything, shit, there's another guy's sperm in your body. *(Pointing to MICHAEL.)* This guy, this stranger, the most intimate thing between a man and a woman and I'm right out of the picture. It's—it's—it's like you cheated on me.

LINDA: You're fucking kidding me.

SCOTT: It's what a man does, it's his contribution to the fertility cycle, it's all we got, and it's him, not me. You've been trespassed upon, you've been stained by another man.

LINDA: How dare you.

SCOTT: I feel slightly sick.

He gulps down his drink, sees MICHAEL.

No offence, man.

MICHAEL: No, no.

LINDA: Oh to be a man and not have to deal with such inconveniences as pregnancy. To be able to just stand aside and offer opinions on what you think I should do. Meanwhile, you can just go on with your life, la de da. You feel betrayed, you feel like I cheated on you. Meanwhile, I'm here, swollen, swollen and saddled with the responsibility of a life I've been told isn't mine.

DARAH: Exactly, it isn't yours.

SCOTT: You're the one with all the power, I'm totally helpless. I can't do anything, you can do whatever the hell you feel like.

LINDA: You think I like being in this position?

SCOTT: Actually, I think there is a part of you that does.

LINDA: How dare you. How dare you.

Both couples talk at once.

LINDA: We planned this, I'm pregnant **because we wanted to be**. /

SCOTT: But this wasn't the plan, this was never the plan, if you had ever let me in on your big plan, we wouldn't have had to drive across town at fucking rush hour, and leave Maya with a—fifty dollars later—babysitter.

LINDA: None of this was the plan but now **we have to deal with this as a family**—not—let's pretend this never happened, what a big drag, I wish I was still a bachelor dealio.

SCOTT: I wish I was a bachelor? Who doesn't even call to check in to say what time she'll be home when she's out—out with the ladies night—**making decisions all on her own.**

LINDA: Ladies night? Since when have I ever had a fucking ladies night? I hate ladies nights.

SCOTT: What do I know? I have no idea what you do with your time, **you never tell me anything,** you make family decisions all on your own—I might as well be a bachelor—single bachelor dad, right here.

After LINDA's "because we wanted to be."

DARAH: (*To MICHAEL.*) See? I told you this wasn't going to work out, I knew it, I just knew it, / I had this feeling, and you got my hopes up, "**no ifs no ifs no ifs no ifs**."

MICHAEL: **Nothing's decided here**. We haven't even discussed this yet. We're just beginning the conversation.

DARAH: **Relax, you said, don't worry, you said**. Don't worry be happy. **If you don't think positively—**

MICHAEL: **And you didn't, you refuse to think positively.** You always do that, you are the most dark—most black—**little**—**rain cloud**—I have ever met. No matter how sunny it is, you'll find the clouds. You make the clouds appear **because you will them**.

DARAH: Are you actually telling me that I made this happen because I wasn't a sunny blue sky? Because sometimes there actually are clouds? Because sometimes it actually rains? Because sometimes things actually get wet, soaking soggy sobbing wet?

LINDA just glares at SCOTT and they are silent. DARAH and MICHAEL realize SCOTT and LINDA are listening to them. Awkward pause.

MICHAEL: What about dinner? We should serve dinner.

DARAH: How can you even think about eating?

MICHAEL: Our guests may be hungry.

SCOTT: Sure, I'll eat chicken.

MICHAEL: Okay.

SCOTT: *(Looking at LINDA.)* Bring on the bird. Normally I can't eat meat in front of Linda, makes her feel alone in her beliefs, but hey, all rules are out the window tonight. I've missed chicken.

LINDA: The chickens don't miss you.

SCOTT: It's just one chicken.

LINDA: It's never just one chicken. It's genocide for chickens.

SCOTT: You can't use the word genocide for chickens.

DARAH: It's not chicken, it's capon.

SCOTT: What's the difference?

MICHAEL: They are a boutique bird, very specialized. You have to order one in advance.

SCOTT: Why so special?

MICHAEL: It's a castrated rooster. The farm we ordered it from uses an ancient technique of removing the testes by hand.

SCOTT: Fancy. Castrated rooster. Do they hold a bris?

MICHAEL: Apparently it's the absence of the male hormones that makes the meat more juicy and flavourful.

SCOTT: How fitting, no male hormones.

DARAH: It's a delicacy.

LINDA: Ew.

MICHAEL: (*To LINDA.*) Sorry, so sorry. I shouldn't have mentioned the—We have salad and cake…I can serve. Shall we all move to the table?

SCOTT: Why not? About time I get to eat meat. Makes me feel more like a man. Distract me from this hell that is my life. Give me some blood.

LINDA: You aren't the one in hell. I am.

SCOTT: Don't pull rank. This affects me too, you know.

LINDA: You have no idea what I'm going through.

SCOTT: I have no idea about anything apparently; you've been lying to me for months.

LINDA: Lying isn't a fair word to use for this.

SCOTT: Lying is lying no matter what the situation is.

MICHAEL: Please please please, let me serve you dinner. I'm sure we're all hungry. We'll all feel better with something in our bellies. (*Gestures.*) Linda, I'm going to make you some fusilli pasta with a black olive pesto. We'll start with the salad and then move on to the mains. *(To SCOTT.)* You'll get your bird, my man, never fear. The table…Please.

MICHAEL makes a grand gesture towards the table—like a waiter in a fancy restaurant. SCOTT moves to the table. LINDA and DARAH stay put.

MICHAEL: Scott, why don't you help yourself to more wine.

SCOTT: Thanks, man.

SCOTT goes into the bathroom, MICHAEL exits to the kitchen.

DARAH: I am dying for a child. Infertile is too clinical a term for how I feel. Maybe I always was, I don't know. Maybe even if I had started at twenty-five I would still have had problems getting pregnant. I'll never know.

(To LINDA.) But now finally, finally our embryo took. This was going to be the one, the fifth round, there are so many stories of successful treatments with the fifth cycle. And we've been waiting four months with no word from you, no idea what was going to happen to our embryo that actually survived. And you want us to give you our only chance at a child? I can't imagine knowing that my child was in the world and I wasn't the mother. It would be unbearable.

MICHAEL swings in with plates on his arms like a waiter.

MICHAEL: Salad is served.

DARAH bursts into tears and runs down the hall and goes into the bathroom as SCOTT comes out. LINDA starts crying, too, and stands up, running blindly away, ends up in front of the bathroom door. LINDA tries to get in, but the door is locked. She pulls at it a bit desperately. DARAH opens it, still crying, the two look at each other, DARAH runs upstairs, and LINDA goes into the bathroom and slams the door. MICHAEL watches them.

MICHAEL: *(Beat.)* You want a scotch?

SCOTT: *(Looks over at the bathroom.)* Why not?

MICHAEL pours them both a scotch. They sip in silence.

MICHAEL: Sometimes, sometimes I can see myself without any of this, forget the house, forget the family, just forget all of it—just me. Alone. In an apartment. A bachelor. Cheap rent. Frozen dinners. Sink full of dishes. Just quit everything. You know?

They drink.

You know what kale is?

SCOTT: What? Yeah.

MICHAEL: I've had six years of it. *(Beat.)* And as each year goes by, we somehow keep holding on to this hope that this time it's going to work out—this time it's going to go our way, we can forget all this and get on with our lives, and then it doesn't happen.

SCOTT: This whole thing is fucked.

MICHAEL: I'm in one room looking at a picture of my wife on my phone, trying to keep the ole lineage going and she's in another room with a nurse, her legs held apart with stirrups.

SCOTT: We should be able to fuck—fuck and mate, reproduce and hunt—we should be able to have babies strewn across the country—it's supposed to be easy for us, right, an afterthought—we're the nice guy if we stick around. My dad never had to know the graphic details of his wife's reproductive system—nothing's sacred anymore.

MICHAEL: But when this happened…finally there was something tangible, a breakthrough, like it might actually be possible to rise above the train wreck and walk again.

SCOTT: Your rise is our train wreck.

MICHAEL: We can turn this around, I know we can. People can do superhuman things and be better for it.

SCOTT: There's no way we can turn this around.

MICHAEL: If this doesn't go through, if it's not a go…it's going to be fighting at two A.M. and eating in silence, feeling like we're never going to smile again, hating every family on the street pushing a stroller, hating playgrounds and diaper commercials. Sitting in the clinic waiting for the doctor to save your life, and I'm snapping at people at work because they don't have a fucking clue and it feels like there's nothing else in our lives but this—There's got to be some sort of compromise. C'mon.

SCOTT: I don't want compromise, I want this whole thing to be done.

MICHAEL: There's got to be a way this can work for all of us. There's got to be. Let's make it happen.

SCOTT: We're at opposite ends of the spectrum here, salesman.

Beat.

DARAH comes back in, red-eyed.

DARAH: (*To MICHAEL.*) Did you serve dinner yet?

MICHAEL: No, the capon is still resting. (*Remembering.*) Shit, the pasta.

MICHAEL dashes to the kitchen. DARAH and SCOTT look at each other awkwardly. A beat. LINDA comes out of the bathroom and charges into the room ferociously.

LINDA: I NEED TO EAT. RIGHT NOW. Right right now!

DARAH: Oh! Oh yes! Of course! Um…(*Yelling.*) Michael! Oh, there's the salad, do you feel like salad?

LINDA crosses to the table and falls ravenously on the salad. MICHAEL sticks his head in.

MICHAEL: What happened, everything okay?

DARAH: Linda's hungry! We have to feed her! Right now!

MICHAEL: Oh! Oh yes!…Of course! I—I have your pasta, I'll just grab it.

He nips in the kitchen. DARAH notices LINDA is almost finished her salad.

DARAH: You can have mine too if you like.

DARAH offers her the plate. LINDA nods. MICHAEL swings in with a large bowl of pasta. He presents it proudly.

MICHAEL: Fusilli with black olive pesto, scattered with sundried tomatoes. Fresh pepper, madam?

DARAH: Just give it to her, Michael!

MICHAEL: Oh, sorry! Sorry, here.

MICHAEL places the bowl of pasta in front of LINDA who takes a huge mouthful. They all watch her.

MICHAEL: I hope you like it…

LINDA doesn't answer, chews.

SCOTT: You can't speak to her when she's like this.

MICHAEL: Oh, right, yes, sorry, sorry.

LINDA eats a few more huge mouthfuls and slows down.

LINDA: Okay. Okay.

SCOTT: Tamed the beast?

LINDA: Wow, yeah. (*She eats a bit more.*) Whew, that was…

MICHAEL: Primal.

LINDA nods, relaxes.

DARAH: You feel better now?

LINDA: Starting to.

MICHAEL: Do you want something else? Dessert? We have that cake… (*To DARAH.*) Go get the cake, hon… or fruit? Maybe fruit too. Strawberries? What else do we have—peaches? Do we have any peaches, Darah?

LINDA: I think I'm good.

MICHAEL: Sure?

LINDA: Yeah. It's just like a lion roaring, so loud, I can't hear anything but FEED ME! And I feel like if I don't eat right then I will die, like the baby is screaming at me. But then, it's over.

MICHAEL: You sure you don't need something sweet? For baby's sweet tooth?

LINDA: No, no, I just have to get something in there, and then we're okay again. It's an incredible thing.

DARAH: How old are you anyway?

LINDA: What does that matter?

MICHAEL: It doesn't matter, you don't have to answer that, Linda.

SCOTT: She's thirty-six.

DARAH: Well, my god. You have time on your side. You're a spring chicken.

LINDA: (*To DARAH.*) I know many women who got pregnant at your age. I know women who have gotten pregnant at forty-eight, older even.

DARAH: They're very lucky.

LINDA: (*To DARAH.*) You have the right to do whatever you have to do in order to have the experience of carrying and birthing and nursing your own baby. Isn't it worth doing another cycle so you have the chance to feel primal, like a lioness? Isn't that what you've been trying for, for six years? Isn't that why you've put yourself through it again and again, because you want what you were made for as a woman?

MICHAEL: Yes, / of course, but—

DARAH: But—

LINDA: Then try again—What if this is your time and you miss it? You'll miss the chance to get exactly what you want. You deserve to get what you want. Six times the charm…

DARAH: (*To LINDA.*) How many cycles of IVF did you do?

MICHAEL: Why does that matter, Darah? We don't need to—

DARAH: I'd like to know.

SCOTT: This was it.

DARAH: One? You only did one?

SCOTT: That was the deal, we'd try one cycle, we only had enough for one round. And wouldn't you know…we got knocked up.

LINDA: We?

DARAH: Thirty-six. One round.

MICHAEL: Gosh some people have all the luck—eh?

LINDA: This is the opposite of luck.

DARAH: No one gets pregnant after one round. It normally takes at least three rounds. Did you even do any IUI's?

SCOTT: They said we should go straight to IVF in our circumstance.

MICHAEL: What circumstance was that?—If you don't mind sharing…

LINDA: …I had a cyst. A big cyst.

SCOTT: It was the size of a baseball.

DARAH: But then you got pregnant after one cycle?

SCOTT: Yep. And then the clinic told us they screwed up.

LINDA: It was a serious surgery to remove the cyst.

SCOTT: The first thing she said when she woke up was "steak."

LINDA: I meant seitan steak.

SCOTT: You meant blood, flesh, prime rib steak. From a cow's rib cage.

LINDA: Oh shut up, I was on heavy painkillers.

SCOTT: Truth serum.

DARAH: Unbelievable. You could get pregnant again in a snap.

LINDA: We don't know that. After my surgery the doctor told us it was IVF or nothing.

DARAH: You already have a daughter. It was just the cyst. Your body was made to make babies. Mine, on the other hand…

SCOTT: Well, you did start late.

MICHAEL: Thirty-eight's not late.

DARAH: Some women start at my age now. Or even older.

LINDA: They absolutely do.

MICHAEL: We're certainly not alone here.

SCOTT: If you had started earlier, do you think we would be here having this conversation?

LINDA: Scott, you're being incredibly rude. Please excuse him.

MICHAEL: Thank you, Linda.

SCOTT: I just don't see any point in tiptoeing around the obvious.

LINDA: Darah and Michael have been very open with us about their journey with infertility.

SCOTT: Too many people think they have to have everything perfectly in place, careers going just so, fancy house, haute couture furniture, nine hundred count linens and then they wonder why they can't conceive when they're forty-five?

MICHAEL: She was thirty-eight—thirty-six, even, when we started trying.

DARAH: I'm not even forty-five now.

SCOTT: The point is you thought if you made enough money, you could afford to wait. And then, surprise…Nature ain't working so well anymore. Nature don't wait for nine-hundred count linen.

DARAH: Linen? You think this is about linen?

SCOTT: Five rounds? Got to have cost you well over a hundred grand. Not to mention the IUI's.

MICHAEL: IUI's are cheap.

SCOTT: For you.

MICHAEL: Yeah, well…

DARAH: The past six years have been awful. I've had to go on anti-depressants. I couldn't sleep, I couldn't get off the couch. I had to take time off work. I didn't shower for weeks. All the cycles ruined me. I'm so scarred from all the needles I'll never wear a bikini again.

SCOTT: No bikini! Poor thing.

LINDA: / Scott—lay off it already.

MICHAEL: Okay now /—let's just—let's just—

DARAH: You can have a baby until you die, / okay? Men have it so easy.

MICHAEL: Look, we're getting way / off topic here.

SCOTT: I'm just saying, someone in the third world wouldn't call this suffering.

DARAH: Developing world. We don't say third / world anymore.

MICHAEL: Okay, Darah, okay.

SCOTT: You get my drift. This was all a choice. It was your choice to do so many treatments. Six years of treatments. In that time you could have adopted three babies. Or accepted it wasn't in your cards and moved on. Many do.

DARAH: If I knew I was going to get a baby in the end, after ten cycles—twenty cycles—guaranteed? I would sell my house, live in a flea-ridden slum, beg, borrow or steal to have my baby. If you really want a child, you don't give up. But we don't have that guarantee, and now we have a baby—(*To LINDA.*) You can wake up in the morning and look in your daughter's eyes. We've given up on having a big family. If we could just have one child I would be happy. I don't think that's asking too much, to just want one child, one precious little thing, to share our life with. We just want to be a family, and how can you be a family without a child?

LINDA: But it shouldn't be about us, we should be thinking about what's right for the baby—

SCOTT: Fetus.

LINDA: A fetus that knows me as its mother. When I give birth it will recognize me as its mother. How can you wrench a baby away from its mother?

DARAH: Because you're not the mother. I am. The baby should be with its genetic parents.

LINDA: The baby doesn't know from genetics.

DARAH: But it will. It will. What do you imagine will happen when that baby wants to know who its real parents are? And you say, oh they live on the other side of town in a big, beautiful, empty house that was supposed to be yours?

SCOTT: Here's the best compromise: call this whole thing off and both start fresh.

DARAH: Killing our baby / is not starting fresh.

MICHAEL: How is that a compromise?

SCOTT: Whoa—hold on there, you can't say killing here, that's not fair.

DARAH: Why not? I'm just saying what you're saying in clear terms. We have to admit that's what we're talking about when you say, "call this whole thing off."

SCOTT: First of all it's a fetus, second of all, it was a mistake that shouldn't have happened. You guys pro-life or something?

MICHAEL: We just want our baby to live.

SCOTT: (*To LINDA.*) See? This is why I knew we shouldn't have come. This is crazy. We were put in a crazy situation. Adoption was never on the table for me—

LINDA: Nothing was on the table for you, I've been totally alone dealing with this.

SCOTT: I'm the one who's made Maya her French toast and spaghetti with cheese. I'm putting off meetings and deadlines to pick Maya up from school and take her to dance class and swimming class and sleepovers. I'm the one arranging play dates so she doesn't have to witness mommy staring blankly into space, wearing her PJs all day.

LINDA: I love wearing PJs. I'd wear them everywhere if I could. I wish I was wearing them now.

MICHAEL: Darah has a pair upstairs. We could get them for you—if you want to change?

LINDA: It's tempting…

SCOTT: Linda, I'm saying I don't want this, I don't want a kid this badly—a kid that has no relation to me whatsoever. I told you from the start I didn't want to adopt. If we're going to have another kid, I want it to be my kid, my DNA. That doesn't affect you at all?

He waits.

What about Maya? Don't you care how this will affect her?

LINDA: She wants a baby brother or sister.

SCOTT: I won't stand for it, Linda, that's it, you actually get these guys to agree to adopt, and I—I can't—I won't—I mean this, Linda, I'll split.

He waits.

Really? Nothing? …That has no impact on you whatsoever?

He waits. They all wait.

Unbelievable. Un-fucking believable. You said you would never want to do that to Maya, now, suddenly, you'll do anything for this fetus who isn't even related to you? Do we, your real family, those around you every single day mean nothing to you? All because of this fetus?

DARAH: …Well, I don't know if this affects what you're talking about, but…we won't agree to an adoption, there's absolutely no way, so…

MICHAEL: No—we—

SCOTT: You hear that, Linda?

LINDA is silent a few beats, heartbroken.

LINDA: Not one of you knows what I am going through.

SCOTT: Don't pull that. No, I have listened. I have tried. I can't help that I'm a man but I am a human being. But you have to think of everyone, not just yourself.

LINDA: I'm not one right now, I'm two. I can't think just for myself. I have to think for both of us.

SCOTT: This pregnancy is fucking with your mind, you're not thinking straight. You have to think of the whole picture. Come on, Linda, just do what you came here to do, what you said you were coming here to do.

MICHAEL: No, please—

DARAH: Please—

LINDA: *(To SCOTT.)* I can't end this baby's life.

SCOTT: You did call the abortion clinic five times, you came very close five times.

MICHAEL: You did?

LINDA: Because I was backed against a wall, I was given two doors to walk through and both of them are awful. But I couldn't go through with it. It doesn't feel any different, you can tell me this is not my baby, but I don't believe you, my body says this is my baby, that I'm the mother.

SCOTT: So are you saying you won't terminate, even though these two—the genetic parents are telling you that under no circumstances will they ever let you keep their baby?

DARAH: Never.

LINDA: Don't you understand? It would feel the same as aborting Maya when I was pregnant. I can't.

SCOTT: So then you will be going through with the pregnancy and handing the baby over to Michael and Darah. That's what you're saying?

LINDA: No.

SCOTT: Then what are you planning on doing? We were told you would never win the baby in court. The law is clear, there's no question.

LINDA: Just in our province. The law here is allowing something that other provinces recognize is totally unethical.

DARAH: Unethical?

SCOTT: So you're going to fight it anyway, against our lawyer's advice?

LINDA: Yes.

SCOTT: Linda, think rationally, please, even if I wanted to adopt this baby, it would take years, years to fight this, not only costing us every dollar we have, taking over your life completely, but meanwhile that baby is going to be ten by the time you get an answer from the Supreme Court, and that kid won't want to leave its mommy and daddy, and won't know you at all. So what are you fighting for?

LINDA: I just know this is my baby. I can't be separated from it.

SCOTT: What else will you do? You going on the lam with the baby? Going to hide in Manitoba? You going to leave Maya? Yeah, I guess she's old enough now, she doesn't need a mother. /

Your job is done. Swap one kid for another? Or kidnap her too while you're at it? Pack a few things and take off in the night? Live the life of outlaws?

LINDA: /Stop it. /Stop it.

SCOTT: Surely you had some sort of Plan B.

LINDA: I don't—I don't know.

She looks wildly around and then makes another run down the hall to the bathroom and slams the door. SCOTT follows and stands outside the bathroom door.

SCOTT: Linda? Linda? Come out. Linda.

LINDA: *(A muffled yelp.)* No!

SCOTT: Okay, then I'm coming in. Linda, open the door.

A silence. LINDA unlocks the door. SCOTT opens it and goes in. DARAH and MICHAEL speak in hushed tones.

MICHAEL: I think we've got a chance here.

DARAH: Are you attracted to her?

MICHAEL: What?

DARAH: Are you?

MICHAEL: No, I'm not attracted to her.

DARAH: She's fat.

MICHAEL: She's pregnant.

DARAH: But you can tell she was fat before.

MICHAEL: I wouldn't say so.

DARAH: So you are attracted to her.

MICHAEL: She's carrying our baby, she's our saviour.

DARAH: You don't think my body can bear a baby do you? / You've given up. I am past my prime, shriveled up, dry.

MICHAEL: Darah, please don't do this, not now.

DARAH: You don't believe if we tried again it would happen. Do you?

MICHAEL: All I can think about is our baby, alive and well in her body.

DARAH: You wish you were with her don't you, a fertile woman. Swollen with your child.

MICHAEL: It's your child too. You're being ridiculous.

DARAH: You're drawn to her, I can tell.

MICHAEL: Darah, this is a very difficult situation, don't make it harder than it is, okay?

DARAH: You are, you are because she has your sperm in her. It's a biological draw.

MICHAEL: She has your egg in her, are you drawn to her?

DARAH: It's not the same thing and you know it.

MICHAEL: I would think you would be. A mother's instinct? She's carrying your child. Pheromones or something?

DARAH: It doesn't work that way.

MICHAEL: So you don't feel anything positive towards her? Just that you hate her?

DARAH: (*Pause.*) I just wish it were me.

MICHAEL: I know, I know, sweetheart. (*Beat.*) Are you hungry?

DARAH: No…Yes.

MICHAEL: I'm starved.

DARAH: She's such… she's a veggie Nazi. I mean, come on, she won't let her husband eat meat in front of her?

MICHAEL: Do you think it's rude if we eat?

DARAH: Just grab us a couple of legs from the kitchen, then it's not like we're eating a meal, just snacking…

MICHAEL: Okay…

MICHAEL rushes to the kitchen. DARAH looks at herself in the mirror, turns sideways, sticks out her belly, rubs it, imagining she's pregnant. MICHAEL comes back in, already tearing some meat off the leg with his teeth. He hands a leg to DARAH. With his mouth full…

MICHAEL: It's really good, love.

DARAH bites into it.

DARAH: I don't know why anyone wouldn't eat meat. It's too good.

MICHAEL: Mmm. So juicy. You outdid yourself.

DARAH: I hope it's not a problem that she doesn't eat meat, nutrients wise, for the baby. Maybe she's not getting enough protein?

MICHAEL: Please don't say that to her okay?

DARAH: But what if the baby isn't growing properly?

MICHAEL: Linda looks pretty healthy to me.

DARAH: You don't think she looks a bit bloated?

MICHAEL: Not at all. She's got that pregnancy glow.

DARAH: Shut up. (*She starts to cry.*)

MICHAEL: Darah…come on, it's good she's glowing. It means our baby is thriving.

DARAH: I want to glow.

MICHAEL: It's not fair. It sucks. But some couples don't have anything. We have a glimmer of hope.

DARAH: I'm an old crone with a uterus full of twigs.

MICHAEL: You are a vibrant, sexy woman. Look at the good side, your feet won't swell, you won't lose your figure, you can go scuba diving, while she'll be aching and farty.

DARAH: She's eight years younger than me. We should have started earlier.

MICHAEL: Don't go there. We need to stay upbeat here.

DARAH: I don't care, we should have. I hate us for not starting earlier. You should have insisted. You didn't care—what was it to you?

MICHAEL: You know how much I regret it.

DARAH: Not as much as me. She's all rosy cheeked and—and in bloom—all shiny and I'm a dried up—skinny—barren witch.

MICHAEL: You're about to be a mother.

DARAH: I just feel like if she does this, and as she gets bigger and bigger, I'm going to feel worse and worse.

MICHAEL: No we'll be getting more and more excited… our baby will be getting closer and closer to us.

DARAH: And what will I say to people? I'm expecting a baby when I'm clearly not?

MICHAEL: Don't tell them anything. You don't owe anything to anyone.

DARAH: And then all of a sudden we have a baby? Out of the blue? They'll think we adopted. They'll think we adopted a crack baby.

MICHAEL: Who cares? Who cares what people think? We'll finally have our baby, our dream come true.

DARAH: But what if one day it says—"Don't tell me what to do—you didn't give birth to me!"

MICHAEL: That's nuts, a kid would never think that. What about all the adopted kids, you think they say that to their mothers?

DARAH: But she's right, I won't have a connection to the baby at all, it won't know me as its mother, she's right, she's right, it's all wrong, its not natural. It's circumventing the natural order of things.

MICHAEL: What do you want to do, go in there and tell them forget it? Call it off, game over? Give her our baby? Is that what you want? Just forget the whole thing? I want our baby, I want this baby, I'll take whatever I can get, however we get it, no it's not perfect, none of this has been what we thought it was going to be, but I want a baby. I want a family. Everyone talks about the woman, everyone sympathizes with you and your dilemma—this has killed me, I'm walking around half a man, I'm dying to be a father—and no one has ever said anything to me about how hard it must be for me, not even you.

Long silence. The bathroom door opens. LINDA and SCOTT come out holding hands. MICHAEL grabs the capon bones and tries to shove them under the coffee table, but capon spills everywhere. DARAH and MICHAEL desperately try to pick all the meaty bits up and MICHAEL shoves the capon in a napkin under the coffee table. A silence.

LINDA: I'll do it.

Stunned silence for a moment.

DARAH: Do you mean…sorry, are you saying…that you'll carry our baby to term…and and then…

LINDA: Yes.

DARAH: And then…we'll have a baby?

LINDA: Yes.

SCOTT: It's a fucking terrible idea.

LINDA: May I have some cake?

DARAH: Yes, yes of course, anything!

MICHAEL lunges forward to hug LINDA, they hold onto each other for a few moments.

MICHAEL: Thank you. You are…incredible…just…thank you.

DARAH: Oh Linda…

LINDA: It's a gift, it's my gift to you.

DARAH: A gift…You are…beautiful.

MICHAEL: Yes…

MICHAEL can't help but hug Linda again.

DARAH: You really are…thank you thank you.

MICHAEL: (*To LINDA.*) You're incredible, just…incredible.

SCOTT: Incredible.

DARAH and MICHAEL embrace.

DARAH: We're having a baby.

MICHAEL hugs LINDA again, then includes SCOTT in the hug. DARAH leans on MICHAEL, trying to join in.

MICHAEL: Thank you, thank you—you are…our angel—our angels. / I am so so grateful…so grateful.

DARAH: You have—we are forever indebted to you.

MICHAEL: What you're doing, it's… *(He tears up.)* phenomenal. Unreal.

DARAH: I know, I know, someone pinch me…finally, a family.

LINDA: The cake?

MICHAEL: / Yeah! The cake!

DARAH: Yes, yes, sorry! I'll bring it out now. Scott, did you want cake too or…You never got your dinner…can I serve you up some capon?

SCOTT: Yeah, I'll have some bird.

DARAH: Wonderful, wonderful.

DARAH rushes to the kitchen.

MICHAEL: (*To LINDA.*) Would you like more Perrier or juice or…

LINDA: Scotch.

Beat.

MICHAEL: Sorry…you want some Scotch?

LINDA: A few sips…

MICHAEL: Sure, of course, definitely. It's a celebration after all. On the rocks or neat?

LINDA: Neat.

MICHAEL: You got it. Another, Scott?

SCOTT: Bring it on.

MICHAEL: Excellent. I'll give you a bottle to take home.

SCOTT: We'll need it.

MICHAEL pours the drinks and hands them to LINDA and SCOTT. DARAH comes in with the cake and a dessert plate with a fork on it. She notices the scotch and glares at MICHAEL. LINDA, meanwhile, takes the whole cake from DARAH and the fork off the dessert plate and starts eating. DARAH notices.

DARAH: Eat the whole thing if you want, Linda. You need the calories. Scott, your dinner is coming.

DARAH goes back to the kitchen. LINDA takes a fork and stabs it into the cake and slowly eats it throughout the following.

MICHAEL: (*To LINDA.*) You are truly our angel. My god. What you are doing for us. I owe you my life. I just hope I can find a way to thank you because saying thank you feels so trivial, there should be a hundred ways to say thank you, like the way the Inuit have a hundred words for snow. Thank you doesn't cut it. I give you a drink and you say thank you, and now all I can say is the same thank you when you've agreed to bear my baby? When you are making me a father? We need more words, we need more words for gratitude, it's pitiful. How do you thank someone who has saved your life?

SCOTT: You save their life.

MICHAEL: That's it, that's it, *(To LINDA.)* I have to save your life. How can I save your life?

LINDA looks at him. A few beats.

LINDA: I don't know.

MICHAEL: We were at the end of the road, Linda, destined to be childless, it just wasn't working for us, we waited too late, our parts don't work anymore, or maybe they never did, whatever, we were just out of luck. And then you showed up. I know this isn't what you wanted, it's an impossible situation, but I mean this, when you walked in the door tonight, I felt something shift. I saw light all around you. I know it sounds like hooey but it's true. I hope you are okay with me saying this, but (*He looks towards the kitchen.*) we needed you. You are young and strong. *(Looks towards the kitchen again, whispers.)* And fertile. Scott, you have an incredibly special wife.

SCOTT: She goes above and beyond…

MICHAEL: Yes! Talk about karma, you're going to come back as a queen, royal blood, an empress. You'll own a country or something.

DARAH comes in with the capon, holds it out proudly for SCOTT to see.

DARAH: Here it is sir, your coq au vin.

SCOTT: Yeah, thanks.

DARAH places the capon on the table and dishes him up a plate.

MICHAEL: See? You say thanks to capon, and I have to use the same words for what Linda has done for us? English is limited, too limited.

DARAH hands SCOTT his plate. He chows down.

DARAH: It's so true. Linda, honey how are you doing?

LINDA: *(Looks at SCOTT's plate, to SCOTT.)* Could you, go somewhere else to eat that?

SCOTT: Sure, I'll keep the bird company. *(He moves to the table.)* Hey, pal.

LINDA: Disgusting.

DARAH: So...you like the cake?

LINDA: Yeah, before the smell of flesh got stuck in my nostrils, I couldn't stop eating it.

DARAH: I used beet juice for colouring. Organic beets. Some purists think you shouldn't use beets for colour, because it doesn't produce the correct shade, but I'd rather use beet juice than red food dye any day. Food colouring is supposed to be terrible for you, and there's good iron in beets. *(Beat.)* God, I can't believe I'm sitting here talking about beets. Can I get you anything else? A nice glass of cold milk maybe?

LINDA: No, just cake.

DARAH: I'm so sorry you had such a hard first trimester. But it's been better? You're feeling better?

SCOTT: The second trimester is usually the honeymoon period but you couldn't exactly call this a honeymoon...

LINDA: Actually, I am feeling better.

SCOTT: Physically. Emotionally it's been...well, maybe things will change now that you've made a decision, for yourself.

LINDA: A decision for everyone.

SCOTT: Whatever.

MICHAEL: It's going to be great, Scott, I promise you.

DARAH: Well, that's good news at least. The physical part, I mean.

MICHAEL: It will be my life's goal to make this a honeymoon for you, Linda…you deserve the royal treatment…You should go to that spa, what's that one, honey, the one for women only?

LINDA: Oh, I love it there.

MICHAEL: You should both go.

DARAH: (*Unsure.*) Mm-hmm…

SCOTT: Female bonding.

MICHAEL: We'll set up a date in the next few weeks. You wear pregnancy so well, Linda. Your hair is so luscious. And your skin…roses and silk…

LINDA: Oh, thank you.

DARAH: Some women just blow up and look haggard and sallow and their hair goes grey.

MICHAEL: Pregnancy becomes you.

SCOTT: She looked good before, too.

MICHAEL: I bet, I bet.

DARAH: And your doctor said everything's fine right? You don't have to take any precautions, or anything?

LINDA: My midwife says my health is great.

SCOTT: You have a midwife?

MICHAEL: Wonderful, wonderful.

DARAH: Well, I just wanted to make sure you didn't need more protein in your diet or something… you know, being a vegetarian I just don't know if—

MICHAEL: She's fine. She's obviously fine.

SCOTT: You have a midwife. Jesus.

LINDA: Yes.

MICHAEL: How does it work, midwives can deliver in a hospital, or it's transferred to a doctor at that point?

LINDA: Midwives can deliver at hospitals…

SCOTT: But with your midwife, you'll want to be at home for the birth of their baby, won't you, honey?

LINDA: …Yes I will.

DARAH: Oh. So…you had Maya at home?

SCOTT: We planned on it. But we had to be transferred to a hospital—and Maya was just too comfortable in there.

DARAH: You aren't worried about it this time? Being so much older?

LINDA: You're only considered high risk after age forty.

DARAH: Everyone says over thirty-five is more risky.

LINDA: That's a dated statistic.

SCOTT: Well, there's always c-sections.

LINDA: You know I would never agree to a c-section.

DARAH: Leave that up to your doctor.

MICHAEL/SCOTT: Midwife.

Pause. LINDA rubs her belly.

MICHAEL: Are you feeling it right now?

LINDA: A little.

MICHAEL: Do you—do you mean it's kicking already?

LINDA: Just starting to feel the flutters.

SCOTT: Flatulence.

MICHAEL: Could I…?

LINDA: What? Oh…

DARAH: Oh, Michael, no, we shouldn't, that's too…

MICHAEL: Oh, sorry, I don't mean to…

LINDA: Okay, yes…

MICHAEL: Really? You don't mind?

LINDA: Please.

MICHAEL sits beside her and gingerly puts his hand on LINDA's belly.

LINDA: Feel that?

MICHAEL: I think so…here?

LINDA: That's it.

MICHAEL: Oh my god, incredible…Hi, baby…it's Daddy…it's Dada…

LINDA: *(To MICHAEL.)* It moved a bit more when you said that, did you feel it?

MICHAEL: Yes, yes, hi, hi, my little one…can't wait to meet you…

SCOTT: What a happy family.

DARAH: Would you…um, do you mind if…

LINDA: Uh, okay…yeah…

DARAH and MICHAEL switch places on the couch and DARAH puts her hand on LINDA's belly. MICHAEL snuggles DARAH while she waits to feel something.

MICHAEL: Feel it?

DARAH: …No.

LINDA: It's very subtle.

MICHAEL: *(Moving DARAH's hand.)* Try here. Feel it?

DARAH: No. Why does everyone feel it but me?

SCOTT: I didn't feel anything.

DARAH: Do you think there's something wrong? Should we call the doctor?

LINDA: No, it's just early on.

MICHAEL: Say something, put your lips right up to her belly…maybe it will move again.

DARAH: *(Timidly.)* Hello, hi…do you hear me? I'm your mother, I'm your mom. Mommy. I'm your mommy. Mama. *(Beat.)* No. Nothing.

MICHAEL: It's still early, Darah. You will soon. *(Beat.)* We'll have to call your parents tonight.

DARAH: Oh my god, my parents—my parents will be over the moon. *(To LINDA.)* They'll want to meet you.

MICHAEL: They'll love you. They'll throw a big party to honour you.

DARAH: Absolutely. The-sky's-the-limit party.

LINDA: They sound sweet…

SCOTT: You want a party?

LINDA: Maybe.

MICHAEL: Watch out, they'll try to adopt you.

DARAH: They will too. (*To MICHAEL.*) And we'll call your dad.

MICHAEL: Right, right, tomorrow.

LINDA: (*To MICHAEL.*) Uh, maybe I'll have just a splash more of that scotch.

DARAH: Do you think that's wise?

MICHAEL: Everyone seems to be relaxing a bit more about booze during pregnancy. I've seen my fair share of women drinking wine looking like they are about to give birth the next day.

DARAH: But that's wine…antioxidants. Hard liquor… is…not.

LINDA: A few sips isn't going to do anything.

SCOTT: Then you've probably hit your limit already.

He takes the scotch MICHAEL offers LINDA out of her hand and takes a long sip.

MICHAEL: Do you need a little massage or something, Linda? Your feet? Pregnant women love to have their feet massaged, don't they?

SCOTT: They really swell up those last couple of months.

LINDA: Oh no, thanks…well…maybe…okay, yeah.

MICHAEL: Yeah?

LINDA: Yeah.

MICHAEL: Take off your shoes, lady!

DARAH: Michael…

LINDA takes off her shoes. MICHAEL kneels down in front of her.

SCOTT: Uh, if you need a massage, I'll do it, Linda.

MICHAEL: No-no—I insist. At one point I considered becoming a masseur.

DARAH: When was that?

MICHAEL: In my undergrad.

DARAH: Your dad would have never allowed it.

MICHAEL: Yeah, yeah, I know. *(To LINDA.)* How's that, Linda? Too hard?

LINDA: Feels great…heaven.

DARAH: Well…that's…

MICHAEL: I'm just going to…

LINDA: Yeah.

A bit of a pause as SCOTT and DARAH look on.

DARAH: Did you want some cake, Scott?…Scott?

SCOTT: Uh…what?

DARAH: Cake? Did you want some? Linda seems to be…

SCOTT: Oh, yeah…sure.

DARAH: I'll just get you a fork then.

DARAH gets up and goes to the kitchen, still looking at them.

LINDA: I don't know the last time I've had my feet massaged.

SCOTT: You could have just asked me.

LINDA: But you hate massaging.

SCOTT: No I don't.

LINDA: You get bored.

SCOTT: No…I just—

MICHAEL: You have to concentrate on your breathing, it's like meditating.

MICHAEL and LINDA breathe for a bit together while SCOTT watches. DARAH comes in with the fork.

DARAH: Oh. I didn't think to bring a dessert plate. You don't need a dessert plate do you?

SCOTT: No.

DARAH: Good. We're all very comfortable now.

She hands the fork to SCOTT and pours herself some scotch. SCOTT eats cake. DARAH drinks. They both watch the massaging.

DARAH: Well, at least I can drink.

LINDA laughs.

LINDA: Oh, my toes are ticklish.

MICHAEL: Sorry! I'll go harder—breathe.

SCOTT: *(Glancing at LINDA for a moment before he turns to DARAH.)* You'll qualify for maternity leave now, won't you?

DARAH: Yes…I guess I will.

SCOTT: Pretty sweet deal.

DARAH: Well, I've earned it.

SCOTT: Didn't say you didn't.

LINDA: *(To MICHAEL.)* Thank you, that was wonderful, truly, the best I've felt in months.

MICHAEL: My pleasure. Anytime. Seriously, anytime. Hey…I know this is silly, but, would you mind if I took a picture?

DARAH: Michael—

MICHAEL: It's such a momentous night—I'd love it for it to be captured.

DARAH: You're so…

MICHAEL: I know, I'm sentimental, I can't help it. *(To LINDA and SCOTT.)* Do you mind?

LINDA: You want to take a picture of us?

MICHAEL: If that's okay.

SCOTT: Here, why don't I take the picture of all of you?

MICHAEL: No, no, you're part of this too, Scott, we're all in this together.

SCOTT: No, no, I'm not…where's the camera?

MICHAEL: Could you grab the camera, Darah? I think it's in my study, on the shelf?

DARAH: Okay then…

DARAH leaves. MICHAEL takes out his phone and snaps a quick one of LINDA.

MICHAEL: Sorry, couldn't resist.

LINDA: Oh, I probably have cake all over my face.

MICHAEL: You look gorgeous, doesn't she, Scott? That pregnancy glow…

SCOTT: Sure.

MICHAEL: I hope you don't mind me saying this, but pregnancy has got to be the sexiest thing. Nature at work.

LINDA: Oh, please.

MICHAEL: It's true, it's true. Am I right, Scott?

SCOTT: It does bring out the curves…

SCOTT rubs LINDA's shoulders awkwardly. She shrugs him off. MICHAEL snaps a photo of the two of them.

MICHAEL: I'll send you copies of these.

DARAH returns with the camera.

Thanks, hon. Go sit next to Linda.

DARAH sits next to LINDA and poses.

Beautiful, you both look beautiful. Do you want to get in there, Scott?

SCOTT: No, I'm on the outside here. I'll take it.

MICHAEL: Okay okay.

MICHAEL sits on the other side of LINDA.

MICHAEL: Would—would it be okay if we put our hands on your belly?

LINDA: Uh, okay, I guess…

MICHAEL: Thank you so much. Darah?

He indicates for her to put her hands on LINDA's belly. She reluctantly does.

MICHAEL: First family photo.

SCOTT snaps.

SCOTT: Classic.

MICHAEL: Scott, you should be in here too. I can set up the automatic timer.

SCOTT: No, I'll just take the photos.

MICHAEL: C'mon, Scott, we should all be together.

SCOTT: You guys are the main players here…

MICHAEL: Just one shot, you're part of this family too.

SCOTT: Uh, I don't think so.

MICHAEL: C'mon.

SCOTT: No.

DARAH: Maybe that's enough photos for now anyway.

MICHAEL: Just one more…*(To LINDA.)* I know it's still early days, but would you mind raising your shirt a little?

LINDA: Oh—uh…

DARAH: Michael, no.

SCOTT: Even more of a classic.

DARAH: It's too much, Michael, Linda, please forgive him…he's…

LINDA: Why not, right?

MICHAEL: Oh, you are so cool.

LINDA raises her shirt, MICHAEL puts his hand on her belly. DARAH stands up and moves away.

SCOTT: You want to get in there, Darah?

DARAH: That's okay…

SCOTT: Say cheese.

MICHAEL/LINDA: Cheese.

SCOTT takes the picture.

LINDA: Okay then…

MICHAEL: I just can't believe we're going to meet him—or her—in less than six months. I know this is soon and everything, but / I can't help but ask—

DARAH: Michael, let her relax.

LINDA: It's okay…

MICHAEL: I just wondered, about the possibility…do you think you might be okay with us being at the birth?

LINDA: …I don't know.

DARAH: Let's not talk about this right now, Michael.

SCOTT: But you should be there. *(To DARAH.)* The midwives will want to lay the baby on your belly, so it will pull itself up to your breasts.

DARAH: Oh…that's…

MICHAEL: Amazing. Wow.

LINDA: I—I need to think about it.

MICHAEL: Of course, of course.

SCOTT: *(To LINDA.)* God, remember Maya's face when she was born? Those black eyes looking around, such a pretty baby.

LINDA: Yes…

SCOTT: Remember she kept sticking out her tongue? This little tongue darting in and out of her mouth. She did it for months, to the point that we were worried she had a problem, but then suddenly one day it just stopped. Mysterious creatures.

MICHAEL: Magical.

SCOTT: Maya and Linda were glued to each other for the first month—skin to skin. I barely got to hold Maya. *(To LINDA.)* You'll need a few moments alone with the baby to say goodbye.

LINDA: Yes, I think so…

SCOTT: You going to make a spaghetti sauce with the placenta again?

LINDA: I don't know…

DARAH: You ate the placenta?

MICHAEL: I've heard of people doing that but I always thought it was a myth. What did it taste like?

SCOTT: Sort of like filet mignon and liver.

DARAH: I don't know if I could eat human flesh.

LINDA: You don't have a problem eating animal flesh.

DARAH: It's different if it's your own species.

MICHAEL: But, if you're vegetarian, it isn't wrong or something?

LINDA: I didn't kill it. It's part of me and part of the baby.

SCOTT: You should both eat some of the placenta… Linda will need to for her postpartum but really—it's part of you too.

MICHAEL: Maybe we should…

DARAH: I'm not eating it.

SCOTT: Speaking of postpartum—

LINDA: I don't want to talk about it.

SCOTT: Yes, but—

LINDA: Stop it.

Pause.

MICHAEL: Well, we would be honoured if we could be present at the birth…but of course…it's your prerogative, Linda, whatever works for you.

DARAH: But, we'd love to come with you to an appointment with your midwife, or an ultrasound, so we could see the progress of the baby.

LINDA: The baby is fine.

MICHAEL: I'd love to see the baby move…but only if that would be okay, Linda?

LINDA: Yeah, uh, I don't know.

DARAH: *(To LINDA.)*…Do you think you're a bit pale?

LINDA: No.

MICHAEL: Not at all, you're blooming.

DARAH: Are you taking any prenatal supplements?

LINDA: I get enough vitamins in my diet.

DARAH: But really you should also be taking calcium and vitamin B, they're so important.

LINDA: I was fine for my last pregnancy.

MICHAEL: Can't get better proof than that, can you?

DARAH: Well, I hope we're able to come to a few of the appointments, it might make us feel more, included—it would be nice to be part of it, in some way.

LINDA: You're getting the baby.

DARAH: I just meant, we may want to figure it out, what the schedule might look like you know... looking ahead these next five plus months.

DARAH looks at MICHAEL.

When we look at the contract we can decide on exact dates...

LINDA: Contract?

SCOTT: What kind of contract are you talking about?

DARAH: Our lawyer drew one up for us, just so we all know what's what.

LINDA: But you didn't even know if it was going to happen or not.

MICHAEL: Just to get something on paper. Stan—that's our lawyer—thought we should, to be prepared. You know lawyers, love to dot their I's and cross their T's before they even get into bed with someone.

LINDA looks at SCOTT.

LINDA: Lawyers are vultures.

SCOTT: Kimberley wasn't a vulture, on the contrary. She just told us the laws, she didn't write them, it's not her fault it wasn't what you wanted to hear.

LINDA: She took our money and did nothing.

SCOTT: And now we're dealing with this alone.

DARAH: Oh, you don't have a lawyer currently?

SCOTT: No.

MICHAEL: Maybe ours can recommend one for you, if that's not a conflict of interest or anything. He's the city's top fertility and surrogacy lawyer, probably the country's best in his field.

DARAH: No...he's just very smart...and nice.

MICHAEL: Darah loves Stan.

LINDA: Stan's a surrogacy lawyer?

MICHAEL: Fertility law really, that's his specialty. He is incredibly thorough...he's intent on making sure that we're protected.

LINDA: Protected? If anyone needs protection now it's me.

SCOTT: Which is why you shouldn't have fired Kimberly.

MICHAEL: I meant protecting us from the clinic. We all need to make sure that we get properly compensated for what happened.

LINDA: But you're getting what you wanted. You've won.

Uncomfortable pause.

SCOTT: Anyway, we don't need a lawyer right this minute. We can find someone appropriate after we've looked over the contract ourselves. Do you have a copy?

DARAH: Yes.

LINDA: Here, in the house?

MICHAEL: Yes.

LINDA: I'd like to see it.

SCOTT: I'd like to see it too.

DARAH: Fabulous.

MICHAEL: All right.

MICHAEL gets it from the shelf under the coffee table and hands it to LINDA. It is a long document.

MICHAEL: You just tell us if there's anything you don't feel comfortable with…

LINDA starts to scan it.

LINDA: This is a surrogacy contract.

SCOTT: That is what you're doing, Linda.

LINDA: *(Reading.)* Hereinafter called the "Gestational Carrier." Gestational Carrier. You can't even use my name?

MICHAEL: It's just the formal nature of the contract. We can get Stan to put your name instead, no problem.

DARAH: Absolutely.

LINDA: *(Reads.)* "The Gestational Carrier agrees to avoid extended travel." Well, that's out, we've booked our tickets to India.

DARAH: India? …In the next five months?

LINDA: They have a saying: "A barren woman has been cursed by God, and is being punished for the sins of a prior life."

DARAH: I'm sorry, I don't follow.

LINDA: Key research for my next project, about the crisis of infertility across the world.

MICHAEL: Jesus, and we thought we had it bad.

DARAH: Can't you wait till after the birth?

MICHAEL: Darah—

SCOTT: After the birth won't be a good time for our family in general…

DARAH: I just worry, it's so far…what if you get sick?

LINDA: I won't cancel, it's all set up, galleries are booked, interviews, it's all planned.

MICHAEL: No problem, no problem, India, you are so inspiring, Linda.

DARAH looks upset, LINDA scans the contract.

LINDA: Amniocentesis at twenty weeks? I don't think so.

SCOTT: Yeah, she's not into that.

DARAH: We would like to know the health of the baby, beforehand—

LINDA: So if we found out it had Downs, you'd want me to abort it?

MICHAEL: No no—not at all…there was a kid with Downs in my elementary school—Gerald—he was great.

LINDA: If you want the test it means you're planning to terminate. There's no other reason to do the test.

DARAH: All my friends did it—just so they could be prepared, to know what they're in for.

MICHAEL: We want our baby, no matter what.

SCOTT: No one *wants* a retarded kid.

LINDA: Retarded?

SCOTT: / You know what I mean.

MICHAEL: People with Downs are very loving.

LINDA: I won't be doing amniocentesis. A baby is a baby.

MICHAEL: That's great, we have no problem with that, (*Hands her a pen.*) cross it out if you like.

LINDA does, with a big X, and continues to scan. DARAH sends MICHAEL a warning look—and mouths: "Don't."

LINDA: (*Reading.*) 'The Gestational Carrier will not nurse the child.' But, I have to nurse the baby, it's vitally important it gets my colostrum.

DARAH: That's impossible. The baby will pick up on your pheromones, it will cause confusion. That's a standard clause.

LINDA: My body will be producing milk for the baby, it's part of the cycle.

SCOTT: You can't nurse their baby, Linda.

LINDA: It's liquid gold, you expect me to just let it go to waste? Let this baby go without crucial antibodies?

SCOTT: I was raised on formula.

MICHAEL: I was too.

LINDA: Because your mothers were brainwashed into thinking breast milk was inferior. We all know now that it's imperative to support their immune system.

MICHAEL: But, I'm perfectly healthy...

LINDA: That has to be part of the deal for me, I can't just let my milk dry up. Even two weeks of breastfeeding can make an incredible difference.

DARAH: Two weeks? Are you serious?

LINDA: A month would actually be better...

SCOTT: Linda, there's no way.

DARAH: Breastfeeding equals bonding. It will confuse our baby. It'll think she's the mother. It'll never take a bottle after that.

MICHAEL: That is a worry.

LINDA: *(To SCOTT.)* I breastfed that baby in Sierra Leone.

DARAH: Sorry, what baby in Sierra Leone?

SCOTT: But that was different—

LINDA: He needed milk, I was still breastfeeding Maya, so I nursed him.

SCOTT: But it was in an orphanage. That baby didn't have a mother.

DARAH: Exactly, this baby has a mother.

LINDA: Don't you care about your baby's health? Your breasts will be dry and my breasts will be full of milk. I'm sorry, I can't waste what my body is naturally providing.

SCOTT: So donate your milk to a milk bank. You still got that pump, right?

DARAH: There you go. That's a great idea, Scott.

SCOTT: Thank you, Michael.

LINDA: That's ludicrous. Why would I donate my milk when it is perfectly composed for this baby?

SCOTT: It's too complicated, Linda.

DARAH: No, no way. Michael, she can't.

MICHAEL: ...we may have to draw the line there, Linda.

LINDA: You expect me to make the biggest sacrifice a woman can make—You should be thanking me for wanting to nurse this baby.

Long silence.

No one knows what to say. LINDA paces, then holds up the contract.

This is—this is bullshit. It's completely one-sided. Protection. Protection from your Gestational Carrier. Gestational Carrier!

MICHAEL: It's a stupid way to phrase it/—we don't think of you like that.

LINDA reads aloud.

LINDA: The Gestational Carrier agrees that she is entering into this Agreement with the intention of *providing a service.*

MICHAEL: That's just generic / phrasing—cross it out.

LINDA: The Gestational Carrier agrees to give birth *at a Hospital.*

MICHAEL: We've discussed that / just cross it out—cross it out.

DARAH: Wait—I want to wait on this one /—Michael—no.

LINDA: I'll give birth anywhere I want, I may decide to give birth in an art gallery if I feel like it.

SCOTT: Don't put it past her.

DARAH: An art gallery /—what are you talking about?

MICHAEL: *(To DARAH.)* Whatever, whatever, who cares where she gives birth?

DARAH: Safety? Hygiene? / Privacy?

LINDA: The Genetic Father and Mother *shall not* be responsible for any expenses relating to emotional or mental conditions / or problems of the Gestational Carrier.

MICHAEL: That's a bit severe, / I can see how that might appear—Cross it out. We don't agree with that at all…

LINDA: The Gestational Carrier agrees to abortion in the case of severe fetal abnormality.

MICHAEL: No—no—we /—don't want you to abort—

SCOTT: Now see, that one I agree with.

LINDA: I knew it, I knew it. It's Nazi eugenics—life unworthy of life.

DARAH: Nazi eugenics? That's insane. We should have just waited till Stan / was here.

LINDA: Stan? Fuck Stan. *(Reads.)* The Gestational Carrier *shall have no* parental rights or obligations of any child / conceived—

MICHAEL: Just rip up the contract, rip it up. / Rip it up… rip it up…

DARAH: No—no!

LINDA: —and does not desire to have any formal communications with the child after delivery. So I'm your fucking surrogate. I am your vessel. Your child was conceived within the glass and I am the live creature who has agreed to incubate your child.

MICHAEL: Not at all, not at all. Those aren't our words. Stan wrote it—that's what lawyers do—crossing his I's and T's. He doesn't get it. We didn't get it. But now we've met you, it's totally different. Just rip it up. Here…

MICHAEL grabs the contract from LINDA.

DARAH: No, Michael—don't!

MICHAEL rips up the contract.

MICHAEL: There, see? Done. Okay? It's gone. It's out of the picture. It was all wrong, all of it. Forget you read it, forget all of it. It was a mistake, a terrible mistake.

LINDA: The very fact that you had that, waiting under your coffee table, says it all.

DARAH: But what do you expect us to do? Just go on blind trust? For all we know, you could stay in India, have the baby and never return.

LINDA: I expect you to do anything I damn well please. I have agreed to separate myself from this baby that I am growing, for you, to go through the worst pain in the world. I am giving you your first born, for fuck's sake. We're in fucking Rumplestiltskin. You should give me your life in return.

MICHAEL: Anything, anything you name it.

LINDA: I want your comfort, I want your life, I want your house.

MICHAEL: You want our house? You can / have our house.

SCOTT: *(To LINDA.)* I don't want their house.

DARAH: We can't give her our house.

MICHAEL: I don't care about the house, who cares about the house? / We can move.

SCOTT: I don't want your house.

MICHAEL: We'll buy you a house just like ours.

SCOTT: I don't want a house like yours.

MICHAEL: Any house you like.

SCOTT: I like my own house.

MICHAEL: *(Under.)* Fuck.

LINDA: This whole night, you've been tiptoeing around me, offering me cake, taking my picture, acting like you care, meanwhile you're waiting for the moment to strip me of my humanity with this toxic contract, and your first-class lawyer making sure you and only you are protected.

MICHAEL: / No, no, not at all—

LINDA: Armed and ready. Lawyer Stan just wants me to shut up and deliver, he's there to protect you because you don't want to even think about the fact that I am carrying "The Child"—*(To DARAH.)* You don't even want to witness the birth because it will be a stinging reminder that "The Child" is not born from you.

DARAH: That's not true, you're misinterpreting.

MICHAEL: We're so grateful—

LINDA: That contract exists to divorce surrogates from nature. To make me sign away my rights to my instincts. Because you are all terrified of my bond with "The Child," because no matter how you try to conceal it, to deny it, nature is occurring. A woman is pregnant, and the mother instinct is so powerful, it needs sixty-seven stipulations on a contract to suppress it.

DARAH: That is totally unfair. Many women have great relationships with their surrogates.

LINDA: Fuck you for having your perfect life at my expense. Fuck you for finally getting it all. You have the house, you have your career and now you have your baby. Check that off the list. I've seen mothers like you for years; for you, it's a paid vacation. Fuck you and your maternity leave.

DARAH: Most women have maternity leave in this country.

LINDA: *(To SCOTT.)* And fuck you for not being on my side—never once through this whole thing have you said—"Whatever you need to do trumps what I need, because it's your body. I'll support whatever you choose to do, we'll work it out." You should have said that to me! *(To DARAH and MICHAEL.)* I can't divorce myself from the natural burst of love occurring every moment carrying this baby. It's a trap, it's a trap—I—I hate it, I hate it—I don't want to be me—I don't want to be me, I want to be Stan, god I want to be Stan, no, no, I want to be the-the-the bus driver, no—I want to be the bus, just the bus, just a stupid bus, and I hate the bus—no—I want to be the road—tar—just tar, black, flat, nothing-nothing—I—I—I can't breathe. I can't breathe—

She bends over.

SCOTT: Linda?

MICHAEL: Linda? Sweetheart?

DARAH: Oh my god. We should—should we—oh my god.

MICHAEL: Linda, Linda listen to me, do you hear my voice? Do you? Linda, look at me, look at me—breathe, breathe—it's going to be okay. That's right that's right, beautiful, beautiful *(Beat.)* You're okay—you're okay—you're breathing… you're breathing…breathe…breathe…

LINDA: …I can't—I can't…if this baby lives, I can't live without it. (*Pause.*)

I—can't live without it, and I can't keep it.

Silence.

SCOTT: Let's go. It's too much, it's all been too much.

SCOTT gets her coat, LINDA is shell-shocked.

MICHAEL: Yes, you should go home, we don't need to make any decisions tonight, we have time… sleep on it, call us tomorrow…or take a few days…whatever you need…

SCOTT tries to help LINDA into her coat.

LINDA: Don't touch me.

SCOTT: Don't touch you?

MICHAEL: We're—we're going to figure this out. We—we just need more time, we all just need more time.

SCOTT heads to the door, DARAH runs and stands in front of it.

DARAH: No! No. / You don't leave yet.

MICHAEL: Darah!

SCOTT: Uh, yeah…we're leaving. We've been here way too long.

DARAH braces herself against the door.

DARAH: No. *(To LINDA.)* You selfish—selfish woman /—you are selfish.

MICHAEL: Darah, please!

DARAH: I don't care—I said it, someone had to say it. You've been sucking up to her all night, like she's one of your goddamn clients.

MICHAEL: What are you saying? No, I haven't—

SCOTT: Yeah, you have.

SCOTT tries to get past DARAH but she puts her arms out and presses herself against the door.

MICHAEL: Linda, please, don't listen to her, she's—she's upset—

DARAH: *(To MICHAEL.)* Shut it. *(To LINDA.)* We didn't want this to happen, we didn't ask for this to happen, we didn't set out to find a surrogate. This happened to us. There are women who agree to be surrogates every day out of the goodness of their hearts. You already have a daughter, you already have a family. You judge me and my life and my choices, but you can't for a moment allow yourself to feel an ounce of pity for me? If I had a child already and was thirty-six, and your embryo had survived inside me, I would carry it for you, as an altruistic act. You'll probably get pregnant again next year. Naturally. And you'll forget all about this. My body won't work any more, my uterus won't hold a fetus. You're a healthy woman in her prime. What's it to you to carry a baby?

LINDA: You have no idea what you are talking about because you are not a mother.

DARAH: You are so smug. You gloat in the fact that you are fertile and I am not.

LINDA: I can't. I can't do it.

SCOTT: Let's go.

MICHAEL: No—Linda—please—You are a mother, you can still be a mother here. Why does it have to be our baby or your baby and that's it? It doesn't have to be like that. It can be all of our baby. Why can't we share?

DARAH: No, no way.

MICHAEL: We can co-parent. People co-parent all the time. I'm a modern man, this is a modern predicament. Let's go with it. Let's make this a modern family. We can figure it out. You can nurse. We can give the baby a bottle. We can do it all.

DARAH: That's insane. That's completely insane. I can't even begin to—I can't even imagine, sharing, what?

MICHAEL: Like—like a timeshare thing—

SCOTT: It's not a condo, you fucking psycho.

MICHAEL: Linda, could you consider this?

LINDA: I—I—I don't know…

SCOTT: I'll tell you right now, no. It's out of the question, out of the question.

MICHAEL: Why can't it be all of us?

DARAH: It's absurd.

MICHAEL: But in time…we can all… / I know we could…

SCOTT: *(To MICHAEL.)* You really think "no" doesn't apply to you.

MICHAEL: Linda? Please. I just have to know, is this something you could consider?

DARAH: Scott and I are saying no, Michael. Why are you asking her?

MICHAEL: Linda?

DARAH: Stop asking her! I won't share, Michael, I won't.

MICHAEL: *(To LINDA.)* You and me, we could do this.

MICHAEL and LINDA stare at each other, imagining.

DARAH: What are you talking about—you and me, what you and me? Michael?

SCOTT: Linda…

DARAH: What is going on? Could someone tell me what is going on?

SCOTT: This is ridiculous. Linda. Linda.

LINDA: *(To MICHAEL.)* …We can't split a human being in half.

Long pause.

MICHAEL: Then keep it.

DARAH: What? Michael.

MICHAEL: Keep the baby. You have my permission, you can adopt.

DARAH: No, absolutely not, not possible.

SCOTT: We're going now.

MICHAEL: The baby should live, I felt it, it's alive in there. We can't just end it because we can't agree on who the rightful parents are. It's not fair to the baby. Please. You can have the baby. / Don't terminate. Please.

DARAH: NO—no way—no fucking way is she getting the baby.

SCOTT: It's a fetus. Fe-tus.

MICHAEL: *(To LINDA.)* Let it live. The baby should live, please, please, keep it, raise it, I don't care, just please.

DARAH: Michael.

SCOTT: Linda said it, she can't do it. It's about sanity. (*Beat.)* We can't get what we want. None of us can. Don't you see that? Don't any of you see that? I'm out.

SCOTT reaches for the door handle behind DARAH, who weakly shuffles aside. He opens the door and leaves. LINDA looks at MICHAEL.

LINDA: I can't...I just, I can't, I'm sorry, I'm...

She runs out of the house.

Silence. DARAH closes the door.

DARAH: How could you even suggest that to her?

You had no place saying that to her, offering her...I can't even say it.

You were ready to give everything up, everything we've worked for, all these years... What about us? Huh? What about us? It's like it was just you and her there.

MICHAEL: How can you let her abort our baby?

Long pause.

DARAH: It's not, it's not a baby—it's not—it's a fetus.

MICHAEL: No. It's a baby.

MICHAEL slides down the wall to sit on the floor, puts his head down. DARAH stares at him and sits on the floor.

DARAH: It just…it just wasn't… *(Beat.)* There has to be… there just has to be a reason… *(Beat.)* Maybe, maybe something's wrong with…the…it's not real, it was never real, it was a mistake.

It was never going to happen.

(Beat.) We should have known…as soon as we were told…we should have known…but…but, it'll work next time, it will…

Long pause.

I'm starving.

MICHAEL just looks at her.

DARAH stands up, goes to the table, takes the capon, and places it on the floor in front of them. MICHAEL just looks at it. She grabs hunks of meat with her hands, and starts eating, savagely, shoving the meat in her mouth, as much as she can fit in.

Lights out.